THOSE WHO REMAIN:

What It Means to Be a Survivor

THOSE WHO REMAIN:

What It Means to Be a Survivor

Ellyn Sanna

 Mason Crest Publishers

THOSE WHO REMAIN:
What It Means to Be a Survivor

MASON CREST PUBLISHERS INC.
370 Reed Road
Broomall, Pennsylvania 19008
(866)MCP-BOOK (toll free)
www.masoncrest.com

Because the stories in this series are told by real people, in some cases names have been changed to protect the privacy of the individuals.

First Printing
9 8 7 6 5 4 3 2 1
ISBN 978-1-4222-0449-8 (series)
ISBN 978-1-4222-1462-6 (series) (pbk.)

Library of Congress Cataloging-in-Publication Data

Sanna, Ellyn, 1957–
  Those who remain : what it means to be a survivor / by Ellyn Sanna.
      p. cm. — (Survivors--ordinary people, extraordinary circumstances)
  Includes bibliographical references and index.
  ISBN 978-1-4222-0457-3 (hbk. : alk. paper) — ISBN 978-1-4222-1470-1 (pbk. : alk. paper)
  1. Loss (Psychology)—Juvenile literature. 2. Grief—Juvenile literature. 3. Psychic trauma—Juvenile literature. I. Title.
  BF575.D35S26 2009
  155.9′37—dc22
                                    2008052181

Design by MK Bassett-Harvey.
Produced by Harding House Publishing Service, Inc.
www.hardinghousepages.com
Cover design by Wendy Arakawa.
Printed in The Hashemite Kingdom of Jordan.

CONTENTS

Introduction

Each of us is confronted with challenges and hardships in our daily lives. Some of us, however, have faced extraordinary challenges and severe adversity. Those who have lived—and often thrived—through affliction, illness, pain, tragedy, cruelty, fear, and even near-death experiences are known as survivors. We have much to learn from survivors and much to admire.

Survivors fascinate us. Notice how many books, movies, and television shows focus on individuals facing—and overcoming—extreme situations. *Robinson Crusoe* is probably the earliest example of this, followed by books like the *Swiss Family Robinson*. Even the old comedy *Gilligan's Island* appealed to this fascination, and today we have everything from the Tom Hanks' movie *Castaway* to the hit reality show *Survivor* and the popular TV show *Lost*.

What is it about survivors that appeals so much to us? Perhaps it's the message of hope they give us. These people have endured extreme challenges—and they've overcome them. They're ordinary people who faced extraordinary situations. And if they can do it, just maybe we can too.

This message is an appropriate one for young adults. After all, adolescence is a time of daily challenges. Change is everywhere in their lives, demanding that they adapt and cope with a constantly shifting reality. Their bodies change in response to increasing levels of sex hormones; their thinking processes change as their brains develop, allowing them to think in more abstract ways; their social lives change as new people and peers become more important. Suddenly, they experience the burning need to form their own identities. At the same time, their emotions are labile and unpredictable. The people they were as children may seem to have disappeared beneath the onslaught of new emotions, thoughts, and sensations. Young adults have to deal with every single one of these changes, all at the same time. Like many of the survivors whose stories are told in this series, adolescents' reality is often a frightening, confusing, and unfamiliar place.

Young adults are in crises that are no less real simply because these are crises we all live through (and most of us survive!) Like all survivors, young adults emerge from their crises transformed; they are not the people they were before. Many of them bear scars they will carry with them for life—and yet these scars can be integrated into their new identities. Scars may even become sources of strength.

In this book series, young adults will have opportunities to learn from individuals faced with tremendous struggles. Each individual has her own story, her own set of circumstances and challenges, and her own way of coping and surviving. Whether facing cancer or abuse, terrorism or natural disaster, genocide or school violence, all the survivors who tell their stories in this series have found the ability and will to carry on despite the trauma. They cope, persevere, persist, and live on as a person changed forever by the ordeal and suffering they endured. They offer hope and wisdom to young adults: if these people can do it, so can they!

These books offer a broad perspective on life and its challenges. They will allow young readers to become more self-aware of the demanding and difficult situations in their own lives—while at the same time becoming more compassionate toward those who have gone through the unthinkable traumas that occur in our world.

— Andrew M. Kleiman, M.D.

Chapter One

BEFORE
AND AFTER

On October 21, 1966, life changed forever.

You and I may not know that, but the people who live in the tiny Welsh town of Aberfan live that fact every day. Even if they weren't born yet on that fall day, the events of more than forty years ago is the axis on which the villagers' existence still turns. Aberfan is a village of survivors. That reality is the framework of their identity.

THE TIP

Aberfan was a mining village. For nearly a century, miners had been digging coal from the mountains that circle the village. The National Coal Board ran the mines, gouging the valuable ore from the earth and dumping the waste **slag** in an enormous mound on the mountainside. The villagers called this pile "the tip."

Tips are all over the mountains of South Wales, scarring the green slopes with heaps of black rubble. During hard times, villagers picked through the slag for bits of usable coal

to burn. Children sometimes played on their slopes.

But in Aberfan, most people had always hated the tip. Rain washed black sludge from the heap of slag down into the village streets; the tip's sides slipped and heaved, like a monster stirring restlessly in its sleep. Since the village school stood on the hillside below the tip, people worried; they wrote letters to the National Coal Board, asking that the tip be moved. Still, the tip had always been there, as long as the villagers' remembered, as long as their oldest grandparents had been alive. It was ugly, it was ominous, but it was a fact of life.

THE DAY THE TREES SCREAMED

On the morning of October 21, people in Aberfan were going about their normal business. Stephen Andrews, the school caretaker, had gotten up early to shovel a load of coal into the school's furnace. He cleaned the bathrooms and then headed home for his breakfast with his wife and two sons. Malcolm was eight, Kelvin was ten, and both were hurrying to get ready for school. It was the last day of school before mid-term vacation, and school would be dismissed early. Like most of the children in Aberfan that morning, Malcolm and Kelvin were excited. They kissed their baby sister good-bye and ran out the door.

In a house high on the hillside, another villager, Mrs. Dinnage, looked down over the mist-filled valley. The fog hid everything from her sight: the village below, the tip above, everything but the power lines that stretched between two poles in front of her house and then disappeared into the thick mist. As Mrs. Dinnage looked out her window, she noticed that the power lines were vibrating, then jumping up and down, like a jump rope that's being swung. "William, come look," she called to her husband. "The wires are shaking. What do you suppose is causing that?"

While the Dinnages were puzzling over the mysterious movement of the power lines, most of Aberfan's children were now in school. They had assembled in the central hall for announcements and prayers; they had sung "All Things Bright and Beautiful" together; and now they were in their classrooms.

Allyson Lewis was in the first grade, filling out a worksheet, when she heard a huge crash. "Get under your desks!" her teacher shouted. The walls were falling, Allyson remembered years later; the cloakroom folded up on top of the classroom.

Gaynor Minett, an eight-year-old in another classroom, was working on an arithmetic assignment when she heard "a tremendous rumbling sound." She remembered later that "all the school went dead. You could hear a pin drop. Everyone was

The rescuers at work with pickaxes, searching for survivors.

petrified, afraid to move. Everyone just froze in their seats. I just managed to get up and I reached the end of my desk when the sound got louder and nearer, until I could see the black out of the window."

Down the hall in another classroom, students were standing around their teacher's desk when the room went suddenly dark. Mr. Williams, the teacher, looked out the window and saw an enormous black wave rushing

The corner
of the school
building is
shown here
buried beneath
debris.

toward the school. "Run to the far side of the wall!" he shouted. Some of his students hurried to obey; others stood frozen.

Stephen Andrews, the school caretaker, was just leaving his house to go back to work when he heard the noise. "It was like a great sea rushing against a wall," he said. "I could see it break right over the school." He shouted to his wife to get the baby and run.

Then he ran to the school, his heart pounding, afraid of what he would find.

Little David Jones had also been running to school, worried because he was late; he didn't want to get in trouble with his teacher. Just as he reached the schoolyard, he saw the building collapse under an immense black flood. He couldn't understand what was happening; all he knew was that he was late, and he needed to get to his classroom, no matter what. "The trees were crying," he remembered later. "All I could hear was the screams as the trees broke."

Inside the school, Mr. Williams looked down and saw his students on the floor, children everywhere. "I couldn't remember any more after that," Gaynor Minett said, "but I woke up to find that a horrible nightmare had just begun in front of my eyes."

What the villagers had always feared at the back of their minds had finally happened: the tip had slid down the mountainside.

A NIGHTMARE

Outside the school, the school nurse who had just gotten to work joined Stephen Andrews. Together, they pulled at the broken walls. "We heard little noises," she said, "not loud screaming and crying but little children noises."

Other villagers rushed to join Mr. Andrews and Nurse Whitford-Jones. They lifted a door and found a little girl whimpering behind it. Near her, a small boy's legs were pinned beneath the rubble. He looked up at the nurse and said, "I'm not dead."

"Of course you're not," she told him and reached down to lift him free.

The students' mothers were at the school now, tearing at the bricks and wood, searching for their children. "We had to break down the front windows and then climb in," said one mother. "We had no tools—we used our bare hands and anything we could find. But there was nothing we could do, between the **slurry** and the water coming down. That was the worst, not being able to do anything. There's nothing as bad as that."

The men joined the women, using spades to shovel the debris. Miners ran down the mountain and went to work. One remembered, "The women were already there, like stone they were, clawing at the filth—it was like a black river—some had no skin left on their hands. Miners are a tough breed, we don't show our feelings, but some of the lads broke down."

Bulldozers joined the diggers. As they worked through the debris, workbooks came to the surface, then a broken doll, children's jackets, a cap. Whenever an arm or a foot was seen, time seemed to stand still. All those who were there remember a heavy silence that hung over the valley. "You couldn't hear a bird or a child," said one man. The crowd of parents held their breaths, waiting. . . .

slurry:
a thin mixture of liquid with a fine insoluble material such as clay, cement, or coal.

Sometimes a child was pulled alive from the wreckage; just as often, the child was dead. After eleven that morning, no one else was found alive. Five teachers were dead and 116 children, most between the ages of seven and ten. Another twenty-eight people died in the twenty houses that had also been engulfed by the dark avalanche that swept down the mountain, breaking a water main, burying everything in its path. At the end of

The villagers searched through the debris, but no survivors were found after the first two hours.

The front of the school was left standing. All those who survived were pulled from this part of the building.

the day, Stephen Andrews' sons were among those found dead beneath the rubble.

For the village of Aberfan, nothing would ever be the same again. The worst thing any of them could have imagined had happened: their children were dead. They were living in a nightmare.

OTHER SURVIVORS

Most of us may never have even heard of the Aberfan disaster. As the decades have gone by, this tiny village has for the most part carried its load of grief alone. The villagers' sorrow and anger, guilt and agony must have seemed like their own unique burdens, something no outsider could understand and share.

It's true that we cannot know what it was like to be one of the villagers' who were left to live in the wake of the Aberfan disaster—but most of us will face our share of loss and trauma at some point in our lives. When we do, we join a community of survivors, a group of human beings that reaches back through time and around the globe, united by the common experience of surviving when others have died. The details of the tragedy vary—some are as dramatic and horrifying as what happened in Aberfan, while others are much more commonplace—and yet survivors all share some of the same reactions.

THE DAY CHILDHOOD CAME TO AN END

On an August Sunday in 1970, thirteen-year-old Anne Dalton had had a good day. She'd played with the kittens on her grandparents' farm; she'd read a thick novel her sisters told her she was too young to understand; she'd picked blackberries and taken notes in her

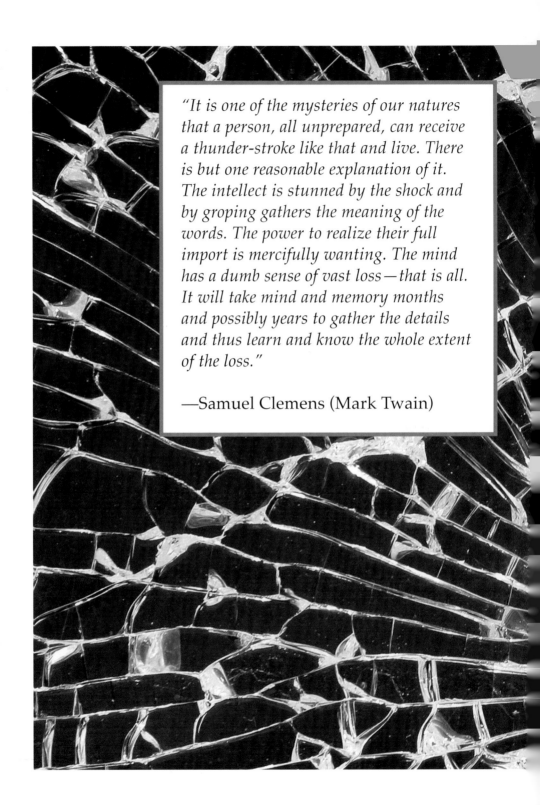

"It is one of the mysteries of our natures that a person, all unprepared, can receive a thunder-stroke like that and live. There is but one reasonable explanation of it. The intellect is stunned by the shock and by groping gathers the meaning of the words. The power to realize their full import is mercifully wanting. The mind has a dumb sense of vast loss—that is all. It will take mind and memory months and possibly years to gather the details and thus learn and know the whole extent of the loss."

—Samuel Clemens (Mark Twain)

Gaynor Minett, the little blonde girl second from the right, was one of the survivors of the Aberfan disaster. Her little brother Carl, sitting on the far right, and her older sister Marilyn, with the dark hair, both died. Michele, the baby here, grew up without any memory of her older brother and sister.

nature journal on a pale green spider; and she listened to her brother's Beatles' albums. Anne's life felt safe and orderly, everything moving along in predictable patterns.

The only thing different about that summer was that her older brother had gone to South America as an exchange student. While he was gone, Anne had taken to listening to his music and reading his books. She enjoyed the chance to snoop through his room, but that Sunday afternoon, it had occurred to her that she missed him. As she played with her grandparents' kittens, she remembers that she looked up at the sun and realized that it was the same ball of fire shining down on Ryan thousands of miles away. Pleased with how profound her thoughts were, she had smiled to herself, glad to be connected to him, glad that he would be coming home in a few weeks.

But that night, Anne woke up from a sound sleep. "Something's happened!" her mother was saying in the hallway outside her bedroom door. "Something awful has happened to Ryan!"

Anne heard her sister Sarah's door open. "But Ryan's in Peru," Sarah mumbled. Anne was thinking the same thing: nothing could have happened to Ryan, because Ryan wasn't there.

But Anne's parents had just received a call from a friend who worked for the state department. The friend was passing along terrible news: in Peru, a plane full of American exchange students had crashed earlier that day, about the same time that Anne had been looking at the sun.

The plane crash in the mountains of Peru claimed the lives of 101 people (including two farmers on the ground). Among those who died were forty-nine American high school students between the ages of fourteen and eighteen. Anne Dalton and her family were just a few of the survivors left behind.

"After my mother woke us up, the next thing I remember," Anne wrote years later in her journal, "was all of us in the living room, my mother, my father, my two sisters. My father was praying. And then, right in the middle of his prayer, his voice cracked. He started crying. I had never heard my father crying before. It scared me. It made me want to run away."

Anne was kneeling next to her mother, with her mother's arms around. "Daddy needs me," her mother told her and pulled away.

"She never really came back," Anne wrote. "That was the last time I got to be a child. It was like a line that was drawn across my life. Before that time, I was this bright precocious kid who thought she knew everything. After that, I was a teenager, full of moods and fears. Everything was different."

AN ORDINARY DEATH

Cheryl Williamson never really knew her younger sister Gwen until they were in their fifties. They had grown up together, their bedrooms right across the hall from each other, but they'd had almost nothing in common. Cheryl was a good student who did her homework every night; Gwen hated school, hated homework, and "goofed off." Cheryl never had a boyfriend until she was in her twenties; Gwen had a steady boyfriend from the time she was fourteen. Cheryl was a "good kid"; "I always did what the grown-ups expected of me," she said as an adult.

The black
river from
the tip was
like volcanic
lava, flowing
down the
mountainside.

Meanwhile, Gwen "was out getting drunk, sneaking out of the house without our parents' permission, spending the night with her boyfriend, smoking pot." Cheryl said, "I didn't approve of her. I didn't tell our parents what she was doing, but I let her know that I thought she was really stupid. . . . Of course I would have liked to have a boyfriend too, but I wasn't jealous of Gwen's. He wasn't all that bright, I didn't think, and I thought Gwen was throwing her life away."

Gaynor Minett's class, the month before the disaster.

As adults, Cheryl and Gwen went their separate ways. Gwen moved across the country, while Cheryl settled down close to their parents. They both married, but they didn't attend each other's weddings. Cheryl had children; Gwen didn't. Cheryl got a job as a nurse; Gwen "had a series of dead-end jobs."

Then, to Cheryl's surprise, Gwen went back to college; she ended up getting a PhD in psychology. "I was jealous of her then, I guess," Cheryl said. "I was supposed to be the smart one. But here I was working as an RN, not making much money, and there was my kid sister, suddenly the big intellectual, making the big bucks in a private practice."

The two women saw each other at family gatherings once every year or two, but that was the extent of their contact until Gwen's husband died. "Suddenly Gwen was calling me on the phone once a month or so. I admit, she'd always made me feel like being snotty. I was usually pretty snippy to her, I think. I'd worked so hard for everything I had, and I felt like she'd just partied and then ended up ahead of me. But how could I be snotty to her now, when her husband had just died? I'd never liked the guy, I always thought the both of them thought they were better than the rest of us. But still, he was dead, and Gwen was obviously heartbroken. And she just kept calling me.

"The next thing I knew, she had gotten a job as a professor at the closest university and was moving back home. She said she wanted to be near us, wanted to get to know my kids, wanted to get to know *me*. There she was, this stranger, suddenly wanting to share my life. We still didn't have all that much in common, but she was my *sister*. She irritated me, the way she couldn't seem to get over her husband's death. The way she didn't even know how to cook, the way she couldn't even pick out curtains for her new house by herself, all that bugged me. But I liked having a sister, someone to talk about Mom and Dad with, someone to laugh with at family gatherings.

Ryan Dalton and the other exchange students boarding the plane before it crashed.

"Her big thing had always been hiking. So this past summer, I promised her I would go hiking with her. Except I never really had time. I meant to. But I was busy at work, so I put it off. 'We'll do it in the fall,' I told her.

"And then she had a heart attack. She was all alone in her house. We didn't even realize she was dead until two weeks later. It was so terrible, finding her.

"I know it was just an ordinary death, the sort of thing that happens all the time. She was young, relatively, but these things happen. But I just can't make it seem right. I feel like everything is different now. I keep thinking that it can't be real, that it doesn't make sense—but it is real. So I end up looking at life completely different, trying to figure it out in a new way. I don't think I'll ever be the same."

THE BLACK DEATH

More than six hundred years ago, a little girl was born in Norfolk, England. Not much is known about her childhood, but little girls of her time followed their mothers through the day, playing with cloth dolls called poppets while their mothers cooked and cleaned and sewed. This little girl was intelligent, and she learned to read and write at home. Like any child, she assumed that the adults in her life would take care of her; life was safe and calm.

And then when she was seven years old, everything changed. The Black Death—the

The mountains outside Cuzco, Peru, where Ryan Dalton's plane crashed.

bubonic plague—had made its deadly way across Europe, and in 1350, it reached Norfolk. Another survivor of this terrible epidemic described the symptom:

> It began both in men and women with certain swellings in the groin or under the armpit. They grew to the size of a small apple or an egg, more or less, and were [commonly] called tumours. In a short space of time these tumours spread from the two parts named all

over the body. Soon after this the symptoms changed and black or purple spots appeared on the arms or thighs or any other part of the body, sometimes a few large ones, sometimes many little ones. These spots were a certain sign of death, just as the original tumour had been and still remained.

Only a month after the first person fell sick in Norfolk, seventy people had died. Within six months, half the population was dead. Once people showed the first symptoms of the plague, they usually were dead within a day. A person could be healthy at suppertime—and dead by bedtime the following day.

The little girl's life was torn apart. Nearly half of all the adults she knew were suddenly gone; she could no longer depend on the grownups to keep her safe, because she knew now that they were weak and **vulnerable**. Most of her friends and the other children in her family were also dead. She never knew who would be still alive from one day to the next. Her life had become a dark and unfamiliar place, filled with the stench and terror of death.

A survivor of this horrifying time described what life was like for ordinary people:

Most of them remained in their houses, either through poverty or in hopes of safety, and fell sick by thousands. Since

vulnerable: susceptible to being hurt or attacked.

The Black Death caused "tumors" or pustules to form in the victim's flesh. Because no one understood what caused the disease, people tried various methods to combat the spread of the terrible illness. Here, a priest is scattering herbs thought to ward off the disease.

they received no care and attention, almost all of them died. Many ended their lives in the streets both at night and during the day; and many others who died in their houses were only known to be dead because the neighbours smelled their decaying bodies. Dead bodies filled every corner. Most of them were treated in the same manner by the survivors, who were more concerned to get rid of their rotting bodies than moved by charity towards the dead. . . . they carried the bodies out of the houses and laid them at the door; where every morning quantities of the dead might

be seen. They then were laid on **biers** or, as these were often lacking, on tables.

Imagine being seven years old and facing this horror. Like Anne Dalton, but at a much earlier age, she must have felt that her child-hood was over. "Before" would have seemed like a happy dream with no connection to the terrifying reality of "after." But she survived. In a world where so many had died, she was one of the lucky ones. She would grow

Sixteenth-century artist Pieter Bruegel created this portrayal of the madness and chaos spread by the plague: *The Triumph of Death.*

biers: stands coffins are placed on before burials.

The bodies of
those who died
from the plague
were carried
on wooden
biers, like that
shown here,
and buried
in unmarked
graves. As the
number of
deaths grew,
all the bodies
collected in a
day would be
dumped into a
single grave.

up and take for herself the name "Julian." The name of the little girl who survived the plague disappeared from history, but Julian of Norwich has endured.

What do all these survivor stories have in common? All the survivors shared a sense that life "will never be the same." The tragic event—whether it was a disaster that affected an entire community or an "ordinary" death in the family—was like a line drawn across the survivors' lives, splitting their memories forever into life before and life after. The people they had once been were changed, gone.

Their new selves were now faced with the hardest task of all: continuing to live when those they loved had died.

"You feel like Humpty Dumpty. You've fallen off the wall and you know all the king's horses and all the king's men are never going to be able to put you together again."

—Joyce Landorf

Chapter Two

FROZEN IN TIME

Each loss is different—and yet each survivor shares some reactions in common. For most people, the first reaction is denial: "This can't be true." Denial is a way to freeze time, to refuse to make the journey from "before" to "after." It's a desperate attempt to hold on to the reality we once knew, to avoid the pain of the new reality with which we're faced.

DON'T TALK ABOUT IT

In Aberfan, the weeks and months after the disaster were shrouded in silence. Life had to continue: there were jobs to be done, other children still to be tended, buildings that needed to be rebuilt. People went forward with the work at hand, but emotionally, for many of the villagers, life had come to a standstill.

"We couldn't talk about the loss for some time," said one bereaved parent. "It threw our life completely off-balance. . . . What can you say? You feel so helpless. You sit there and you can't say a thing."

One of the surviving students remembers, "In those days talking of your emotions was an embarrassment. As a child you felt ashamed to tell someone what you were feeling, even if you were crying. You didn't want them to know you were crying. I only cried when I went to bed in the evenings. If my mother heard me she would come in to see me, but I couldn't talk to her about how I felt—and in the morning I would feel embarrassed. In my family we never discussed what had happened. Nothing was said. Just tears and very quiet. . . . My mother still won't talk about that time. She doesn't want to know. She's blanked it out. It was the only way she could cope."

Another student said, "What happened in Aberfan that day was the dark little secret when we were young and it still is. We knew we must not speak out. We have been quiet for the sake of the other people, those who lost children and those who did not want to hear about what happened, especially from the mouths of their own children. . . . Most of us live in the same small village and have grown up together, yet we all kept everything locked away inside ourselves."

A parent in Aberfan said that his little boy wouldn't talk about what had happened, nor

In the weeks after the disaster, media attention focused on the village of Aberfan—but for the villagers, life had come to a standstill as they grappled with their loss.

would he mention his sister who had died in the disaster. "And the two of them worshipped each other," the father said. "They was always together; slept in the same room, holding hands." The little boy would hide when his parents went to his sister's grave.

A mother in Aberfan said she too had refused to go to the cemetery. Instead, she imagined that her son was away "on a fortnight's holiday with relatives." "If I go up there," she said, "I'll know it is over. As long as I don't, I have some hope."

After her brother's death, Anne Dalton experienced something very similar. "I refused to go to the cemetery with my parents. And I wouldn't talk about Ryan being dead, I wouldn't even think about it. It made me mad if I saw my parents crying. 'You're making Ryan dead every time you cry!' I shouted at my mother once.

The clean-up work in Aberfan was long and grueling.

According to the Mayo Clinic, people of all ages can have post-traumatic stress disorder (PTSD). About 7 percent to 8 percent of all adults—that's seven or eight people out of every hundred—will have PTSD at some point in their lives. In any given year, about 5 million American adults have PTSD.

"Deep inside, I didn't really believe he even *was* dead. After all, I'd never seen the body, just a closed casket. If you'd asked me, I would have said I knew my brother was dead, and I'd have meant it—but meanwhile, every time I was in a crowd somewhere, I was searching the faces, looking for him. I never cried. I didn't feel sad. I was so sure Ryan was really alive.

"A few years ago, my mother told me how much she'd envied my faith. She said she had felt as though my faith in God, in eternal life, was so much stronger than hers that she felt guilty. But it wasn't faith I was feeling. It was just denial. I didn't want to accept that Ryan was really gone, that he wasn't coming back."

Cheryl Williamson didn't want to talk about her sister's death either. "I didn't even want to have a funeral," she said. "I finally gave in, because the relatives were so horrified, but I made sure it was the most impersonal funeral ever. I didn't want it to have anything to do with Gwen. And I shut myself off from everyone, even my best friend, especially my best friend. She would call me, assuming I needed to talk, but that was the last thing I wanted. I couldn't even see her, couldn't answer the phone when I saw her number on caller ID, because I knew she'd expect me to do more than make chit-chat. I didn't *want* to talk."

For the villagers of Aberfan, the black scar lying across their valley was a constant reminder of death.

RELIVING THE TRAUMA

Denial is one way to stop time in its tracks, but memories are another. Some memories

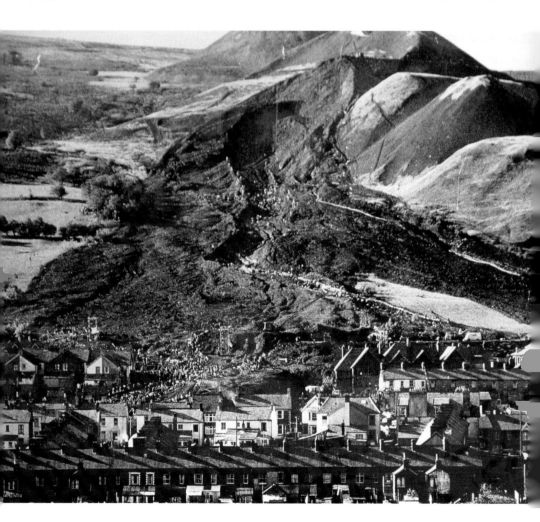

can be a comfort, of course, but for many survivors, memory becomes something they can't control, a trick of their brains that brings back the terror and grief as though it were happening all over again. These flashbacks are one symptom of what psychologists refer to as post-traumatic stress disorder.

Aberfan's doctor said that in the days after the disaster, "The first real thing that happened were the terrible nightmares people suffered, reliving the event time and time again." The doctor prescribed sedatives for many of the town's residents—but if was raining, they refused to take the drugs; they were afraid to go to sleep, he said, afraid of what might happen while they were unconscious. Meanwhile, children in Aberfan slept with their doors open, terrified of being trapped.

Sleep makes our unconscious vulnerable to memories, but when a person is experiencing PTSD, he does not have to be asleep to have a nightmare. A parent of one of Aberfan's surviving children described how his son kept seeing the houses falling toward him

In the months following the disaster, a ruined house still stood, its walls propped to keep it from collapsing.

whenever he walked down the street where the school had stood. "She's a different little girl," another father said of his surviving daughter in the days after the disaster. "She's afraid to go to the temporary school because it looks like the old school building, being red brick like. We send her every day, but she just stands outside and cries or else runs home."

Another father described the night when he identified his daughter's body. "I've never forgotten that. It comes back to me every day.

There's some part of the day that that picture comes back to me and I can never forget that.. . . All those little bodies wrapped in blankets."

REFUSING TO MOVE ON

Facing death is terrifying; rebuilding your life can seem even more frightening. Confronted with such an overwhelming task, our emotions and bodies sometimes respond with a feeling of exhaustion, a bone-deep reluctance to tackle this unwelcome work.

The people of Aberfan experienced this. When author Laurie Lee visited the village a year after the disaster, he found a village still caught in the morning after the disaster. He wrote:

> Fragments of the school itself still lie embedded in the rubbish—chunks of green-painted classroom wall. . . . Even more **poignant** relics lie in a corner of the buried playground piled haphazardly against a wall—some miniature desks and chairs, **evocative** as a dead child's clothes. . . . Among the rubble there also lie crumbled song-books, sodden and smeared with slime, the words of some bed-time song still visible on the pages surrounded by drawings of sleeping elves.
>
> Across the road from the school, and facing up the mountain, stands a row of

poignant: deeply moving to the emotions.

evocative: serving to bring to mind.

One of Aberfan's many graves for its children.

abandoned houses. This must once have been a trim little working class terrace . . . with lace-curtained windows, potted plants in the hall, and a piano in every parlor—until the wave of slag broke against it, smashed the doors and windows, and squeezed through the rooms like toothpaste.

Something has been done to clear them, but not very much. They stand like broken and blackened teeth. Doors sag, windows gape, revealing the devastation within—a crushed piano, some half-smothered furniture. You can step in from the street and walk around the forsaken rooms which still **emit** an **aura** of suffocation and panic—floors scattered with letters, coat-hangers on the stairs, a jar of pickles on the kitchen table. The sense of catastrophe and desertation, resembling the choked ruins of Pompeii, hangs in the air like volcanic dust.

Cheryl Williamson felt a similar *inertia* after her sister's death. "I needed to clean out Gwen's house. It was my job to take care of all the things a person leaves behind, but I couldn't make myself do it. I was just too tired, as though her dying had worn me out. Besides, I didn't want to think about her being gone. I wanted to pretend she had moved back to California, that life was just the way it was before she moved back

emit: issue, send forth.

aura: a distinctive or pervasive quality or character.

inertia: the tendency of a body of matter to maintain its state of rest or uniform motion if not acted on by an outside force.

Cherished Memories of

OUR DARLING SON
BRIAN DAVIES
AGED 8½ YEARS OLD
WHO DIED IN THE ABERFAN DISASTER
21 OCTOBER 1966

SAFE IN THE ARMS OF JESUS

home, that nothing had really changed, that we could all just go on the way we used to. I didn't want to face this huge, ugly hole Gwen had made in my life when she died. So how could I clean her house, handle her clothes, put away all the stuff that was hers? I was just too tired."

Anne Dalton may have been too young to feel the weariness Cheryl described, but she too was unwilling to change the physical world in response to her brother's death. "I didn't want my parents to clean out his room, and when they did, it was one of the few times, I cried. But mostly I was furious with them. It was as though I thought that if we left everything the same—all his record albums, his books, the Middle Earth posters on the wall, his clothes in the closet—one day he would come back. And then life would go back to normal."

Julian of Norwich was also reluctant to move on past the horror that had struck her community. Although she had survived, she could not accept the gift of her health. Instead, she prayed over and over that God would give her a deadly illness like the one that had killed so many of the people she loved. For her, death and sickness had become normal—and she could not accept the new reality of everyday life, a life where she was healthy and alive while so many others were not.

WAKING UP

"I woke up in the middle of the night," Cheryl said, "and it was like Gwen had shaken my shoulder. I'm not saying I think I was visited by a ghost or anything. It was just that I suddenly knew I had to face her death. I'd wasted all the time I could afford with my head buried in the sand, and now it was time to get busy, to face the facts. So I did. It wasn't fun,

Opposite page: Graves can eventually bring comfort to those who are left behind, but in the weeks and months immediately after a loss, some people would rather avoid their loved ones' grave sites. To visit the cemetery means to accept the death of the person they love.

Sometimes the moment when a person is ready to go on with life is dramatic, like finding the end of a dark tunnel; in most cases, it is probably more gradual.

but suddenly I could do it. I wasn't stuck any more, the way I had been."

Anne had a similar moment. "It was years later that I finally accepted that Ryan was dead. I was in college, and the father of a close friend had died suddenly. A bunch of us went to the funeral home, and there he was, this body just lying there for everyone to see. It was the first time I had seen a dead body. I thought it was obscene, unnatural, a terrible tradition. I was so angry I couldn't stay there. I went outside and gagged. And then that night I started crying. At first I was crying for my friend's father, but pretty soon I knew I was really crying for Ryan. I cried and cried, and my roommate put her arms around me and held me. I guess I was making up for all those years when I never cried. I broke the blood vessels around my eyes, I cried so hard. The next day people kept asking me what had happened. I felt stupid saying, 'Well, you see my brother died six years ago.' But that was the first time I really accepted that he was dead. It was as if I'd finally opened my eyes to a reality I'd refused to see all those years. It was awful—but I'd also never felt so light, so full of energy as I did during the weeks after I cried like that. Holding all that back must have been taking so much of my energy all those years. I felt like I'd been sleepwalking and now I was finally awake. And once I was awake, the promise of life after death meant so much more. It was amazing, like this shiny miracle I'd never noticed before."

One of the survivors in Aberfan also grasped the hope of a future life as momentum to propel him past his denial. The little boy who had thought the buildings were falling on him whenever he walked down the street, the same boy who refused to go with his parents to his sister's grave, surprised his father by calling to him one night when he'd gone outside to use the outhouse.

"I heard him call, 'Dad!' 'Ay, what is it, boy?' I said. 'Come out here!' he said. 'Sure,' I said, 'what's the matter?' It was a beautiful frosty night. He said, 'Look at that star there—that's our Sandie, Dad.' 'Sure,' I said, that's our little Sandie.' The boy's all right now." On an ordinary and prosaic trip to the outhouse, for whatever reason, a star spoke of life and hope to the boy—and that was the turning point for him, the moment when he decided to go forward.

Julian of Norwich's turning point came when her prayers were answered: she fell ill and was not expected to live. During her sickness, she had a vision that made her look at her life in an entirely new way. When she recovered, she took a new path for her life, one that connected her to the meaning she had found while she was so sick.

After a tragedy or disaster, survivors often speak of having to find a "new normal." Doing so means they must first let go of the past. Taking that step may happen naturally; others may need help—from their faith, from a counselor, from a particularly beautiful starry night, from some event that shakes them out of their inertia—to become "unstuck" and move forward.

Once they do, they can no longer linger in the moment of loss; they must find the energy and courage to go on. They have begun the long and difficult journey forward into the rest of their lives.

"We find that we have to let go in order to move forward; and letting go means dying a little. In the process we are being created anew, awakened afresh."

—Kathleen B. Fischer

Chapter Three

A DIFFICULT JOURNEY

M oving on after a loss is not easy. Most survivors encounter a series of obstacles in their journey. One of the hardest to get past is guilt.

SURVIVOR GUILT

The fact that the Aberfan disaster's victims were mostly children was particularly hard for the survivors. Adults are supposed to keep children safe; many of the villagers felt they had failed in this most important of tasks. Most of the fathers of the dead children were miners, the ones who had built the tip that slid down the mountain and took their children's lives (although it was actually the National Coal Board that was responsible for the placement of the tip, not the miners themselves). Teachers who escaped from the crushed school building felt guilty for being alive when so many of their charges were not; they had been responsible for the students, and now their students were dead. Even the surviving students themselves felt guilty, simply for being alive.

"I kept asking myself why I hadn't died," said one student. "I blamed myself for allowing my brother and sister to die."

Aberfan's doctor said, "Women who had sent their children who hadn't wanted to go to school that day suffered terrible feelings of guilt. . . . Grief and guilt came in many different ways. There was a strange bitterness between families who lost children and those who hadn't; people just could not help it."

"We didn't go out to play for a long time," said one of the surviving children, "because those who'd lost their own children couldn't bear to see us. We all knew what they were feeling and we felt guilty about being alive."

Even among those who shared the loss of a loved one, there was a hierarchy of guilt. One man in Aberfan was struck harder than the rest: his wife was killed when the slag swept down the mountain and crushed their house; his teenage son was outside the school and was caught by the black avalanche; and his youngest son died inside the school. The other parents in the village treated him with caution and **deference**, guilty they had

deference: courteous respect.

lost only one child when he had lost every-thing.

Cheryl Williamson also felt guilty about her sister's death. "I hated thinking that she was alone when she died. I kept thinking if I'd called her, if I'd gone to see her, if we'd gone hiking earlier in the summer the way she'd wanted, I might have been able to tell she wasn't well, I might have made her go to the doctor, she might still be alive. And then I

The village of Aberfan lies in the shadow of its cemetery. The reminder of death is always with them.

The names of each of the children who died in Aberfan's disaster are listed on this cross. Each child also has an arch. The rows of arches stretch the length of the hillside.

started thinking about all the times I'd let her down, all the times I'd been snitty to her, all the times when I could have gotten together with her but I made an excuse because I was busy or tired or wanted to stay home with my family. I felt like I'd let her down over and over.

"Her colleagues at the university had a memorial service for her, and as I listened to their **eulogies**, I realized how little I'd known her, how little effort I'd made to understand what was important to her, what she was good at. She'd been there my entire life, and I'd taken for granted that she'd always be there. I'd never bothered to appreciate her. And now that I finally did, it was too late. I never even told her I loved her. I mean I think she knew, but I would have liked to have said it. I would have liked to have been there for her more often."

Julian of Norwich must also have felt guilty; why else would she have asked God to strike her with a deadly disease? After all, she had survived when so many around her had died. When that happens, people ask themselves, "Why? Why am I alive when someone who was as good as me or better is dead? I don't deserve to be alive."

"I've carried guilt with me for years," Anne Dalton wrote. "I was alive and Ryan was dead, but I didn't deserve to be alive. I felt as though Ryan had been punished for my sins. I carried the secret of my guilt inside me, hidden from the rest of the world, including my husband. I knew it didn't make sense at a rational level. But when I had miscarriages, one right after another, I felt as though the babies I lost had paid for what I deserved. People would say to me, 'You've had so many hard things happen to you,' but I always felt I'd gotten off easy. Sometimes I felt as though I were creeping

eulogies: speeches or writings in praise of a person, especially a deceased person.

The grave of one of Aberfan's children.

through life, keeping my head down, trying to escape God's notice, the way I used to do in school when I didn't want the teacher to call on me. I was afraid if I did something to bring myself to God's attention, He'd have to punish me finally the way I deserved."

Psychologists explain that survival guilt is a normal and natural reaction after the loss of someone close to us. But it can also be a roadblock that halts our journey back toward

IN LOVING MEMORY OF
ERYL MAI JONES
DAUGHTER OF MR AND MRS TREFOR JONES
IRONMONGERS ABERFAN
AGED 10 YEARS

life; not everyone manages to find a way past this obstacle.

Author and psychologist Robert Lifton writes:

> At the time of the trauma, there is a quick and immediate sense that one should respond according to one's ordinary standards, in certain constructive ways, by halting the path of the trauma or evil, or by helping other people in a constructive way. Neither of these may be possible during extreme trauma. At the very most, the response that is possible is less than the ideal expectation.

In the wake of a tragedy or disaster, most people set standards that are too high for themselves. They hold themselves accountable for failures that no one could have avoided.

According to psychologist Yael Danieli, guilt may also be a way to hold on to our connection to the person we have lost. We may be afraid that if we allow ourselves to let go of our guilt, if we allow ourselves to be happy again, we will be letting our lost loved ones drop into **oblivion**. Our guilt expresses our loyalty to those who are gone. It builds a graveyard inside our hearts and minds, an ongoing memorial to them.

After a loss, guilt also allows us to insist that life is not simply a chaotic and unpredictable mess. According to Danieli, "The idea that one somehow could have prevented

oblivion: the condition of total forgetting or being forgotten.

As an adult, Gaynor Minett Madgwick still struggles to let go of the past. She sits here in her living room, surrounded by reminders of the tragedy that changed her life forever.

what happened may be more desirable than the frightening notion that events were completely random and senseless." If only we had done this or that, we think, then the horrible event could have been prevented. We should have *known*, we say to ourselves. We should have been paying attention, we shouldn't have been so careless, so lazy, so selfish. We would rather put the blame on ourselves than accept that reality is sometimes simply beyond our ability to control. It's less terrifying to let go of our own self-esteem than to face the fact that we live in an uncertain and **precarious** world.

Survivors of the **Holocaust** have suffered for years with heavy burdens of guilt. One seventy-year-old man, the only survivor from his family, told author Lawrence Langer:

> I'm guilty all my life. I'm guilty I didn't save my father, my mother, my sister. I feel guilty, I could have made Aryan papers for them. I'm guilty I tried to talk them into going to Russia, but they wouldn't listen. I'm guilty, I don't want to be richer than my father. I had opportunities to make millions. I always feel guilty. Why should I have more than my parents? Maybe I'm wrong. I'm guilty. I feel guilty all my life.

> In December 1944, when the war started coming to an end, although we didn't know that, or we did not know to what extent—we were taken out of camp and started off to march. . . . It was terrible cold; we had no clothes. Whoever could not walk they shot. We had

precarious: insecure, uncertain, dependant on circumstances beyond one's control.

Holocaust: the mass slaughter of European Jews by the Nazis during World War II.

Holocaust survivors often struggle with both guilt and rage—guilt that they survived when so many did not; rage because of what they were forced to endure.

no food. At night they herded us in . . . a barn. Next morning very early they took us out and we had to march again; we marched for days. And during the march, my brother . . . he could not walk anymore and he was taken from me and shot on the road. . . . We were reduced to such an animal level that actually now that I remember those things, I feel more horrible than I felt at the time. We were in such a state that all that mattered is to remain alive. Even about your own brother, one did not think. I don't know how other people felt. . . . It bothers me very much if I was the only one that felt that way, or is that normal in such circumstances to be that way? I feel now sometimes, did do my best or didn't I do something that I should have done? But at the time I wanted to survive myself,

The villagers of Aberfan had reason to feel bitter; letters were written to the National Coal Board more than two years before the disaster, warning that the tip was a danger to the school.

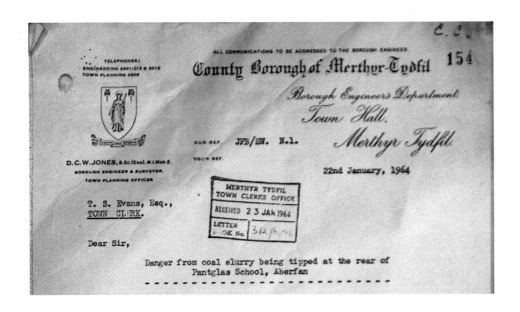

and maybe I did not give my greatest efforts to do certain things, or I missed to do certain things.

Ethel, another Holocaust survivor interviewed by Langer, said, "I always compare myself to other survivors."

I don't feel like I suffered enough. I even always compare my suffering to the suffering of non-survivors. I compare it, measure it. His [suffering] was a ten but mine was only a nine. . . . I [relive the memories]. I need to feel it. When I don't feel it, I feel like I'm numb. . . . Like I got out of Auschwitz and I want to go back. It's like reconnecting with something very real in me, like my **authentic** self. I need to feel that part of me is alive.

authentic: genuine, real.

degradation: a decline to a lower condition or level.

Langer writes, "Ethel perceives her authentic self to be the self which suffers pain and **degradation**. Her authentic self is the self which lived in hell. . . . She perpetually pricks her wound because she never wants it to heal. Ethel will die, as the others died, consumed by Auschwitz." She told Langer, "I always feel like I have to earn my life."

People like Ethel have not gotten past guilt's roadblock; they are still stuck, unable to move forward into the new reality where they now live. "Some people couldn't recover," said Gaynor Minett Madgwick, one of Aberfan's survivors. "They lived, but they might as well have died. Their entire lives were consumed by what happened. They couldn't go on, they couldn't make anything of themselves. Some of them eventually committed suicide. They were the last victims

Money from the disaster fund built the children's memorial in the cemetery above Aberfan. For the parents of the dead children, however, no memorial or money could make up for what they had lost.

of that day in 1966. They just took longer to die."

Guilt like this has a cost, one that is paid not only by the individual but by those around him. It can interfere with his ability to relate

to others; it can submerge family members in a cloud of gloom; and it can prevent him from being able to be a productive member of society.

But psychologists say that guilt can also be constructive; it can be a steppingstone toward a more meaningful life. For the Holocaust survivors, it motivated many of them to bear witness to the inhumanity and cruelty of what had happened, to speak out and educate others. Julian of Norwich joined a religious order and used the rest of her life to help others. Cheryl Williamson said, "I am trying to be more sensitive to others now. I don't want to ever again feel as though I've let someone I love down. I make an effort now to be more careful, to be aware of others'

The Stages of Grief

Elizabeth Kubler-Ross was the first to identify stages in the grieving process. These are the steps most survivors pass through on their journey toward the future.

- denial (This can't be *happening* to me!)
- anger (Why is this happening to *me*?)

- bargaining (I promise I'll be a better person if . . .)
- depression (I don't *care* anymore.)
- acceptance (I'm ready for whatever comes.)

Not everyone experiences each of these stages, and not everyone experiences them in the same order. Sometimes survivors pass through one stage, only to return to it again further down the road.

Coping with Survival Guilt

Psychologist Karen Flood offers these suggestions to survivors who are experiencing guilt:

- Ask yourself how you feel and be as honest as you can.
- Using grief as a period for practicing self-care will help you work toward acceptance of your loss. Ask yourself what you need, so you can express your feelings and soothe your pain. Participate in rituals of grieving and remember to say goodbye. It is important to talk about or think about the deceased and your relationship to them. Write a note, share your thoughts about the deceased, attend a funeral or celebration of life. If you find yourself grieving many deaths, reach out to others with the same circumstance. Build those supports.
- Know how to reach out for help and where to look for support. Most bereaved individuals recover from their loss with help from family, friends and spiritual advisors. However, if you experience persistent feelings of depression or anxiety, professional help may assist you moving through the grief.
- Re-invest energy into once again experiencing life. Some find meaning through community events such as fund raising for research, social activism, and volunteerism.
- Remember that survivor's guilt is an experience to be acknowledged, not a problem to be avoided.

Psychologist Kathleen Nader adds these recommendations:

- Be aware of any desire to self-punish—self-punishment is nonproductive; take positive action instead.
- Be reasonable with yourself. Don't expect more from yourself than what is humanly possible.
- If you truly caused harm to others, be willing to experience embarrassment and any discomfort it takes to make appropriate amends.
- Recognize guilt's function: at its best, guilt serves as a mobilizer to productive action.
- Be aware that guilt may mask other emotions; examine yourself to determine if you are using guilt to avoid other emotions.

feelings. And I tell people I love them. That's something I never did before. I just wasn't comfortable saying the words. But I'd rather feel uncomfortable than feel the regret I do over never saying it to Gwen. It gets easier the more often I say it."

Sometimes, survivor guilt may be anger that's been turned back against the individual, instead of being directed outward. Danieli writes:

perpetrators: those who carry out a crime or other wrongdoing.

From a psychodynamic viewpoint, the Holocaust survivor's guilt may reflect constraints against the expression of rage toward the **perpetrators** of his misfortune, toward the Nazis and their collaborators, and toward parents who

---

Another Perspective on Grief

In Dr. Roberta Temes' book, *Living with an Empty Chair: A Guide Through Grief*, she describes three particular types of behavior exhibited by those suffering from grief and loss:

- numbness (mechanical functioning and separation from others)
- disorganization (intensely painful feelings of loss)
- reorganization (re-entry into a more "normal" social life)

Temes' "numbness" corresponds to the "frozen in time feeling" experienced by Cheryl, Anne, Julian of Norwich, and many of the residents of Aberfan. "Disorganization" for them was full of guilt and anger, as well as overwhelming grief. Eventually, they were ready for "reorganization."

---

failed to provide protection from those torturous events. Instead of expressing rage outwardly, the survivor turns it upon himself. Guilt is the **embodiment** of anger directed toward the self.

embodiment: representation of an idea.

ANGER

"After Ryan died," Anne Dalton wrote, "I talked with another sibling who had lost a sister in the same plane crash. He was so angry at the airlines for causing the crash with their carelessness. I never felt angry at the airlines, though. The parents sued them—the settlement ended up paying for my college education—but it didn't really seem to have anything at all to do with Ryan. Instead, once I finally accepted that he was dead, I was furious with *him*. I didn't even know I was until I was telling my counselor about seeing someone who looked like Ryan, thinking just for an instant that it was him. 'In that instant, what did you want to say to him?' the counselor asked me. 'I wanted to slug him,' I said before I could think. And then I realized it was true. I was mad at Ryan for abandoning me, for leaving me with parents who were depressed all the time, for changing my life forever. It didn't make sense, I knew that—but I had to accept that those were my feelings before I could finally forgive him."

Cheryl Williamson was also mad at her sister. "She should have taken better care of herself. She drank too much, she never went to the doctor. I was so frustrated that I couldn't yell at her the way I would have over something else she'd done, that I couldn't say, '*Now* look what you've done, you idiot!' And then, while I was cleaning out her house, I started feeling angry at her husband. She'd spent so much of her life just revolving around his needs. He'd been unwell for years, and she'd worn herself out caring for him at the same time she was working to support them. He hadn't worked for the past ten years or more before his death. And then

Statue of Julian of Norwich from Norwich Cathedral in Norfolk, England.

she'd been so wrapped up in mourning him. Finally, this year, it should have been her turn to live, to have fun, to figure out who she was without him. And then she never got that chance. 'You selfish jerk!' I found myself saying as I packed his stuff into boxes. 'You never gave her a chance to be anything but your wife.' I felt so angry, I wanted to break all that stuff of his she'd saved so carefully."

The Aberfan survivors were angry too—and with good reason. The National Coal Board (NCB) could have prevented the disaster; letters had been written, warning the NCB the tip was unsafe, but nothing had been done.

Survivors can get stuck in their anger, just as they can get stuck in guilt. But like guilt, anger can also be a force for good. In Aberfan, the villagers' rage united them and motivated them to work for justice. "Whatever happens to me," one father said, "the thing for me to do is to show the world what has happened. I owe that to my family." In the face of his loss, the fight for a disaster fund gave him something to hold on to. It gave him a goal, a reason to get up in the morning.

Survivors' journeys into a new and bleaker future is never easy. But simply staying alive, one day after another, allows time to ease some of the pain. Eventually, survivors can look back and see how far they've come.

"Believe that life is worth living and your belief will help create the fact."

—William James

Chapter Four

THE PERSPECTIVE OF TIME

Gaynor Minett Madgwick is a grown woman now with children of her own, but she still remembers that October day in Aberfan. "It was a horrible nightmare. Bodies lay crushed and buried. I was too dazed to scream or do anything." She was trapped beneath the rubble, her leg and hip crushed. Her grandfather was the one who finally pulled her out.

Gaynor spent months in the hospital after the disaster. She came home to a world that was completely different from the one she had known. Her little brother and her big sister were dead; many of her friends were dead; and her village had become a community focused on loss.

Gaynor Minett Madgwick today.

"For years," Gaynor said, "I tried to block out my memories. No one wanted to hear them. They would have just upset my parents. They were just too painful." But then, when Gaynor was in her early teens, she began to write. Telling her story helped her make sense out of what had happened; it helped her find her place in the world.

Gaynor grew up, married, had a family. She works now helping troubled young people to find their own places in the world. And thirty years after the Aberfan disaster, she finished the book she had begun as a teenager. *Aberfan: Struggling Out of Darkness* was published in 1996. "I wanted the book to help other survivors," she said. "I know from experience that it takes a long, long time to get the fears and frustrations out of the system. Writing the book was my way of healing."

Gaynor's life demonstrates two of the best tools for overcoming a tragedy: creativity and giving back to others.

CREATIVITY

Scientists, **philosophers, theologians,** and psychologists have speculated about the power of creativity. Earlier thinkers attributed the creative force to God or the gods, a force outside ourselves that moves through us. Freud, the father of psychoanalysis, speculated that creativity springs from our frustrations; we **sublimate** our negative emotions in positive action. **Neurologists** tell us that creativity comes from our right brain (while our left brain is more methodical).

Whatever its source, creativity is a powerful tool for healing. Whether we put together words, paint a picture, make music, play a

philosophers: those who study truth, knowledge, and theories about ideas and the state of being.

theologians: those who study God and religious ideas.

sublimate: to divert one's energy from one's immediate desire or goal to a more acceptable or useful goal.

neurologists: doctors specializing in the nervous system and disorders related to the nervous system.

role on stage, sew, build, or simply come up with new ideas, creativity somehow allows us to rise above our sadness and despair.

Scientists have defined creativity as an "assumptions-breaking process." Creative ideas are often generated when we discard **preconceived** assumptions and attempt a new approach or method that might seem unthinkable according to our old thought patterns. In another words, creativity helps get us "unstuck." It moves us forward.

preconceived: formed an opinion or idea before seeing evidence, or as a result of a prejudice.

The ability to make new connections between things is another aspect of creativity. This can help us find meaning in our lives. After the death of someone close to us, life often seems chaotic, a series of random events without meaning. When Gaynor told her story, she found a way to make a pattern out of the events in her life; she made sense out of it. Others in Aberfan wrote poems.

Sheila Lewis, whose ten-year-old daughter Sharon died in the school, said, "I couldn't sleep at all, so I got up and wrote. . . . It made me feel better."

> "In the months after my daughter's death, I filled four notebooks with entries—writing sometimes daily, sometimes only once in several days. I described feeling, the events of the day, occasions of recall, of sorrow and hope. It was a means of moving the grief away, getting it down somewhere else, siphoning it off."
>
> —Martha Whitmore Hickman

Gaynor's notebook where she first wrote down her story.

"Whoever survives a test, whatever it may be, must tell the story. That is his duty."

—Elie Wiesel, Holocaust survivor

An artist expressed his sorrow over the Aberfan tragedy with this drawing, showing a rescuer with one of the children in his arms.

Grief, it seems, must be our lot.
Grief at times seems all we've got.
I must not die and join her yet.
My husband needs me, my children would fret.

It didn't matter whether the poetry was skillful; just giving her thoughts shape with a pattern of words comforted Mrs. Lewis.

"Writing is how I understand life," Anne Dalton wrote. "The thoughts inside my head are often muddled, dingy things—but sometimes when I put them together on paper, I

Creative Survivors

Many composers, singers, and authors who survived
the loss of someone close to them have used their grief
and anguish to fuel their creativity. Eric Clapton, for
example, composed "Tears in Heaven" after his young
son's accidental death from a fall. By singing the song
"Fly," Celine Dion described her emotions after her niece's
death, who died from cystic fibrosis. Paul McCartney wrote
"Here Today" after John Lennon's tragic shooting. Elton
John rewrote "Candle in the Wind" to remember Princess
Diana after her tragic death. Many of the classic books on
grief have been written by authors dealing with their own
grief, as a way of coping with the loss. C.S. Lewis wrote
A Grief Observed after the death of his wife Joy. Writer
Martha Whitmore Hickman created *Healing After Loss:
Daily Meditations for Working Through Grief* following
the death of her sixteen-year-old daughter in a riding
accident. *Safe Passages: Words to Help the Grieving Hold
Fast and Let Go* was written by Molly Fumia as her way
of mourning the loss of her firstborn son. Rabbi Harold
Kushner wrote *When Bad Things Happen to Good People*
in reaction to his son's death.

find patterns there I never saw before. Even
the ugliest, saddest, stupidest feelings, the
old tired thoughts that seem stuck inside
me, change when I put them into written
words."

Julian of Norwich also used writing to turn
her experiences into a gift to the world. The
little girl who survived the Black Death, who

For some people, cemeteries offer a way to express feelings tangibly to someone who can no longer be seen or touched. This stone stands as a gift of love from two of Aberfan's parents to their dead child.

wanted nothing except to get sick and die too, lived to be an old woman. For years she pondered her experiences, and eventually, she put them together in words. Her book, *Divine Love*, was the first to be written by a woman in the English language. Centuries later, theologians continue to praise Julian's intelligence and insights, and ordinary readers still find comfort in her words.

Ideas for Dealing with Grief Creatively

- Create a collage or decoupage to expresses grief using newspapers, magazine, painting, markers, photography, original painting, etc.
- Take photographs to illustrate grief—or encourage hope.
- Make a scrapbook using photographs, schoolwork, drawings, letters, mementos, favorite sayings, and family memories.
- Paint emotions on paper with whatever paints or colors and whatever technique feels right.
- Mold or construct masks with different media to illustrate grief.
- Express emotions using molding clay or in sculpting
- Sew a memory quilt or make a teddy bear using clothes from the person you lost.
- Build an ofrenda or altar.
- Decorate a memory box and fill it with mementos that remind you of the person you lost.
- Built a memorial bench.
- Make anniversary cards, candles, bookmarks, or picture frames to remember the lost loved one.
- Write a poem.
- Write a letter to the person you lost.

Not everyone needs words to be creative, though. "I quilt," Cheryl Williamson said. "I couldn't tell you why it makes me feel better, but somehow it does. Putting pieces of cloth together in a pattern . . . it soothes me. I can't put in words why this helps. It just does. Since Gwen's death, my father has built an

A quilt made by Cheryl Williamson after her sister's death.

entire new room on their house. My mother sits and plays the piano. And I've made two quilts. I wouldn't say we're creative people, though. If any of us were creative, we would have always said it was Gwen. But it's as though her death has given us this strange, sad energy. I'm not sure it makes us happier, doing these things, but it does help us cope. Just to express that energy somehow, to *make* something with it. There's a satisfaction in it, a peace."

> "I have found over the years that my writing has more courage than I do."
>
> —Linda Hogan

Creativity can be expressed in many forms. "Taking care of the cemetery has kept my father strong," Gaynor said. "He goes every day. You'd think that might be **morbid**, but it's not. He's cheerful. It gives him pleasure to make the memorial a beautiful place. It's given his life meaning all these years. For many of the parents, the cemetery is the center of their lives, the core of their hearts, the thing that keeps them sane."

morbid: characterizing an unhealthy or unwholesome state of mind.

GIVING TO OTHERS

"Not all of us have healed," Gaynor said. "Even now, after all these years, there are people I went to school with who are walking around as broken as they were forty years ago. One of the big differences I see is what we've done with our lives. The ones of us who have done fine are the ones who are doing something to give back to the world. We're teaching or doing social work or working in the church. The ones who just sit home feeling guilty and sad, those are the ones who haven't recovered."

Reverend Kenneth Hayes, who lost his son in the Aberfan disaster, worked hard to give back to his community, despite his own loss. He and his wife ran a toys appeal for the village's surviving children. He gave his home as office for the solicitors who filed a complaint against the Coal Board. He spoke often of both his sorrow and his faith, allowing others to share in his strength. Thirty years after the disaster, he told journalists, "As far as I'm concerned now, we've still got two boys. We're only separated for a time. One day we're going to meet. The parting and the loneliness and being without him is terrible, but it's not forever." Reverend Hayes' faith was expressed in his commitment to others. That commitment allowed him to transform his grief into a priceless tool for doing good in the world.

"I always said that Gwen was the bleeding heart in the family," Cheryl said. "She was the one who took in stray cats, the one who worked with troubled kids, the one who married a man with a load of problems. I was the practical one, the cold-hearted one, I guess. But now, it's like I feel I have to do

> "We do not write in order to be understood; we write in order to understand."
>
> —C. Day-Lewis

those things for her, because she's not here anymore to do them for herself. I have to take inside me a piece of her, the piece that reached out to the world. I've even gotten to know her group of friends, this bunch of people I would have once called losers—and who I now realize are unique, loving, interesting . . . and yeah, pretty strange, but yet they're enriching my life somehow.

For Gaynor's father, the children's memorial became the focus of his creative energy. By creating a beautiful place in the children's honor, he found peace and healing.

CHILDREN, COME UNTO ME

The children's memorial in Aberfan combines both creativity and faith to offer comfort to the community.

"Gwen had this thing about helping people be all they can be. It was like it was her only real goal in life, to help others. So I feel like the best memorial I can build for her is by allowing her to change me. To become all I can be. And that seems to mean that I have to be willing to reach out to people I never would have before she died."

THE ONGOING JOURNEY

After a loss, people often find that the life they build is enriched by all that they've learned. Going on with life, however, does not mean that the trauma is erased. People who find the courage to make something meaningful out of their lives still have wounds.

"Here I am, a grown man," said one of Aberfan's survivors, "a tough ex-miner and all that, yet since that day I don't like the dark." Another survivor wrote, "All of us are subconsciously waiting for the alarm to sound again." Still another said, "My abiding memory of that day is blackness and dark. I was buried by that horrible slurry and I am afraid of the dark to this day."

"Certain things scare me that never did before," Cheryl Williamson said. "It's silly, but I'll find my heart pounding for no reason."

Psychologists tell us that post-traumatic stress disorder can spring to life even decades later. But in most cases, the symptoms do fade with time. Another Aberfan survivor said, "For many years after the disaster if I was sitting in an enclosed room and a jet airplane would approach, I would absolutely quake and shiver until it had gone and actually feel the nerves running through my body. I think it also affected my driving as well. I was very aware of the . . . dangers in the environment. But gradually over the years it sort of disappeared and now I'm all right. I can **rationalize** a jet airplane."

rationalize: using reason to excuse behavior, beliefs, etc.

"*Piece by piece, I reenter the world. A new phase. . . . Birds console me by flying, trees by growing. . . . It's like a slow recovery from a sickness, this recovery of one's self.*"

—*Toby Talbot*

An artist's image of what Julian of Norwich might have looked like. After the vision she experienced during her illness, Julian became a hermitess, a woman who shut herself away in a small room attached to a church. Although this sounds like a lonely life, actually, Julian's life was a lot like a modern-day therapist's. She had a window in her hermitage where she would sit, and people came to her seeking counseling. Julian, like other survivors, rose above her trauma by giving of herself to others.

JULIAN OF NORWICH

Anniversaries and special occasions can also resurrect the trauma. "Gwen's birthday is a hard time for our family," Cheryl said. "And Christmas too. All the special occasions where the hole she left becomes more noticeable again."

Grief and trauma have many triggers. Anne Dalton wrote, "I feel that at each stage of my life, I must once again cope with Ryan's death, as though it means something different to me at every milestone. When I fell in love and got married, I was terrified my husband would die. In fact, I knew he would die—all people do, after all, sooner or later—and it seemed unbearable to me. If he was late coming home from work, if he had to fly somewhere, I had his funeral all planned. I'd be a wreck by the time he got home. I drove him crazy. But I was so scared to just enjoy him for fear I'd lose him. Eventually, I realized, though, it wasn't about him — it was about Ryan. I had to spend time all over again coming to terms with my brother's death.

> "As for inflicting our sorrow on other people, one does not want to go around blathering and crying all the time. But perhaps it is our gift to others to trust them enough to share our feelings with them. It may help them deal with some of their own."
>
> —Martha Whitmore Hickman

"When I had my children, that was another trigger that brought it all back to life. I had never before truly realized what my parents experienced. I had lost a brother, but it's very different, far worse, I think, to lose a child. Once I had my own children, I understood that. But it terrified me. How could I bear to live in a world that might take the life of these little people who were so precious to me? How could I possibly ever be happy again when they were so terrible vulnerable? I kept all this to myself—when you're a mother you don't have the luxury of falling apart too much—but inside I was going quietly crazy. I got so I was afraid to go outside—the power lines worried me. I'd be pulling the kids in their wagon, and I'd be thinking, *What if the power lines fall on us?* Driving across long bridges frightened me; I could see so clearly in mind the moment when they'd collapse beneath our car, the children's voices, me trying to get them out, trying to swim with them through the icy water. . . . The world was full of horror. I couldn't cope. I had to go get help eventually from a counselor.

"There have been other smaller, crisis points, where I've needed to confront Ryan's death again, in a new way. I wonder if as I get older I will need to think about Ryan's death in relation to my own—and if that will frighten me or comfort me."

Survivors have traveled a long road. Sometimes they may feel as though they make no progress whatsoever, that they are going in

Flowers in the children's memorial garden in Aberfan remind us that life rises out of death and sorrow.

> "When you find yourself overpowered by melancholy, the best way is to go out and do something kind for someone."
>
> —John Keble

circles, dealing with the same emotions over and over again—but when they look back from the vantage point of time, they can see just how far they have come. Those who do more than merely survive, the ones who go on to truly *live* again, have learned many important lessons along the way. Their stories enrich us all.

Their stories also fascinate us. We love to hear about the person who made it alive out of dangerous circumstances; we get **vicarious** pleasure from tales of courage and bravery in the face of incredible odds. Survivors seem to have cheated death—and death is our ultimate fear.

vicarious: taking the place of a person or thing as a substitute.

The reality, however, is that each of us will die—and sooner or later, each of us will be confronted with the death of someone close to us. When that happens, we can turn to the vast community of survivors and benefit from their wisdom and strength.

"Whatever the wounds that have to heal, the moment of creation assures that all is well, that one is still in tune with the universe . . .

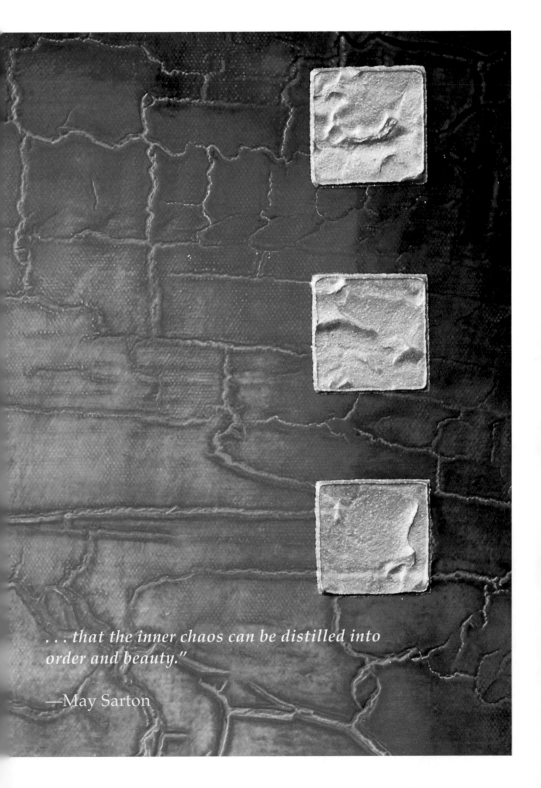

. . . that the inner chaos can be distilled into order and beauty."

—May Sarton

Chapter Five

WE ARE ALL SURVIVORS

We'd all like to pretend we're immune to death. It's something our culture encourages us to believe. We hide death out of sight. We act as though death is abnormal, a rare occurrence that disrupts everyday life. But it's not.

Theologian Marcus Borg wrote:

As numerous studies demonstrate, contemporary mainstream American culture is deeply death-denying. To some extent, this attitude of denial has come about because of changes in our society in this century: the marked decrease in the number of deaths at an early age; the development of specialized professions for the care of the dying and the dead;

emergence:
gradual
beginning, the
act of coming
out.

mobility: the
ability to move
freely.

the **emergence** of geographical **mobility**, with the consequence that most of us live at some distance from aging and dying relatives, including parents; the growth of separate communities for the aging, not only nursing homes but retirement communities. More and more, the aging and the dying do not

Aberfan today.

Tips for Survivors

Follow your health professional's instructions. Although it may take a while to feel benefits from therapy or medications, most people do begin to feel better within a few weeks. Remind yourself that it takes time. Healing won't come overnight. Following your treatment plan will help move you forward.

Take care of yourself. Get enough rest, eat a balanced diet, exercise, and take time to relax. Avoid caffeine and nicotine, which can worsen anxiety.

Don't self-medicate. Turning to alcohol or drugs to numb your feelings isn't healthy, even though it may be a tempting way to cope. It can lead to more problems down the road and prevent real healing.

Break the cycle. When you feel anxious, take a brisk walk or delve into a hobby to refocus.

Talk to someone. Stay connected with supportive and caring family, friends, faith leaders or others. You don't have to talk about what happened, if you don't want to. Just sharing time together with loved ones can offer healing and comfort.

Consider a support group. Many communities have support groups geared for specific situations. Ask your health care professional for help finding one, look in your local phone book, or contact your community's social services system.

Make a resolution. For many people, living through a traumatic event becomes a turning point to make positive changes in their lives and grow emotionally and psychologically. For instance, some people who live through a serious car accident caused by someone under the influence of alcohol may resolve to combat drinking and driving.

(From the Mayo Clinic's Web site, www.mayoclinic.com/health/post-traumatic-stress-disorder/DS00246/ DSECTION=coping-and-support)

insulated:
protected,
separated.

live among us. Increasingly, we are **insulated** from death.

Sooner or later, though, death rips through our insulation. Someone close to us dies. And then we too are survivors.

After surviving a traumatic event, most people are unable to stop thinking about what happened. Fear, anxiety, anger, depression, and guilt are all common reactions. Psychologists recommend that you expect yourself to have these feelings. Be kind to yourself, experts recommend; get enough sleep, eat healthy foods, and don't expect more from yourself than you are capable of doing. Although you may not want to talk about your feelings or even think about what's happened, getting support can help you recover. This may mean turning to family and friends who will listen and offer comfort—or it may mean you seek out a mental health professional. Some people also may find help from their faith community or a religious leader. However you choose to get

"Grief is a tidal wave that over takes you, smashes down upon you with unimaginable force, sweeps you up into its darkness, where you tumble and crash against unidentifiable surfaces, only to be thrown out on an unknown beach, bruised, reshaped. . . . Grief will make a new person out of you, if it doesn't kill you in the making."

—Stephanie Ericsson

Gaynor's memories will always be with her. Here she points to a photograph of the child she once was.

support and help, research shows that doing so helps prevent normal stress reactions from developing into post-traumatic stress disorder. Getting support may keep you from turning to unhealthy coping methods, such as alcohol abuse, overeating, or drug use.

SURVIVORS' WISDOM

"I am a better person, I think," Gaynor Madgwick said. "I would never have chosen to experience this. I would rather have my brother and sister back. But this is what is. I have to live with this my entire life. I will use it to build on, a foundation for something good."

"My life was less painful before," Cheryl Williamson said. "I thought I was in control. Now I know I'm not. But the world seems bigger now, filled with surprises. Some of them

The ancient Greeks thought that creativity came from the nine Muses, the goddesses of inspiration.

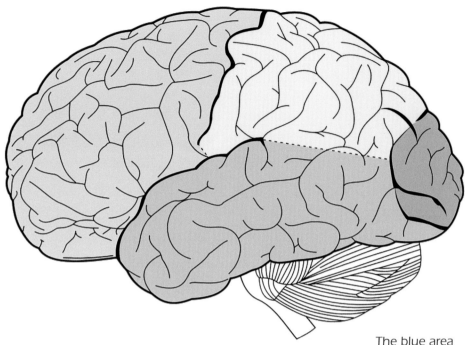

The blue area shown on this diagram is the part of the brain scientists believe is responsible for creativity.

are horrible—like Gwen dying—but some of them aren't, like learning to be friends with her friends. I'm glad she was my sister. I'm glad she'll always be a part of me."

"I learned when I was very young that life is uncertain," Anne Dalton wrote. "I would rather hide from that. But Ryan's death keeps coming back to confront me. I have to look at the world and see past the messages I hear on commercials, that if only I clean my floors

"Suffering breaks our world. Like a tree struck by lightning—splintered, shaken, denuded—our world is broken . . . and we will never be the same again. What will become of us is a mystery."

—Nathan Kollar

A statue of Julian of Norwich stands outside the Cathedral of Norfolk, and her book is still read by people around the world.

> "Out of every crisis comes the chance to be reborn, to reconceive ourselves as individuals, to choose the kind of change that will help us grow and to fulfill ourselves more completely."
>
> —Nena O'Neill

with a certain soap, drink a specific soda, and wash my hair with this particular shampoo, everything will be rosy and happy and safe. Sometimes I'd rather live in commercial-land. But the reality is bigger and more interesting. Facing that reality is like climbing a mountain. It takes effort; it makes the muscles in your legs hurt; your lungs ache from lack of oxygen. It would be easier to just poke along on the level. But the view from the top of the mountain is amazing."

"All shall be well," Julian of Norwich wrote, "and all shall be well, and all manner of things shall be well."

Some survivors have lost loved ones to cancer, AIDS, and other diseases. Others have

> "Loss is a common experience that each person encounters during his or her lifetime. It does not discriminate for age, race, sex, education, economic status or nationality. Loss is a byproduct of being alive."
>
> —Kirsti A. Dyer

Today, the San Jeronimo Mountains, the site of Ryan Dalton's plane crash, lie peaceful and serene in the afternoon sunlight.

lived through natural disasters and man-made catastrophes. Still other people have endured the loss of loved ones to "ordinary" causes: car crashes, old age, everyday illnesses. We can't really compare these events; we can't say one is worse than the other, for in the end, each person's pain is unique.

Whether we are speaking of one of Aberfan's survivors . . . a child from the Middle Ages who survived the Black Death . . . a teenager whose brother died in a plane crash . . . a woman whose sister died of a heart attack . . . or any of the other circumstances that bring death, all survivors have some things in common. They enrich our world as they refuse to let events limit who they are or what they have to offer. They take even the worst pain and use it creatively, to reach out to others; to inspire music, paintings, poetry, and stories; to challenge themselves to play sports, make gardens, invent new things, research new scientific discoveries; to make themselves stronger. They live with hope and courage, taking pleasure in life's many joys, no matter how much hurt they are asked to endure.

RESILIENCY

Psychologists refer to "resiliency" as the capacity to cope positively with stress and catastrophe. According to psychologist Carl C. Bell, people who are resilient have these characteristics:

- resourcefulness

- the ability to attract and use support

- curiosity and intellectual mastery

- compassion for others

- the conviction of one's right to survive

- the ability to remember and invoke images of good and sustaining figures

- the ability to be in touch with emotions, not denying or suppressing feelings as they arise

- goals to live for

- a vision of the possibility and desirability of restoration of order

- the need and ability to help others

- the ability to conceptualize and imagine possibilities

- learned helpfulness (rather than helplessness)

Looking down from the cemetery, over Aberfan's valley.

In an interview with author Cathy Caruth, psychologist Robert Lifton, an expert on trauma said:

> Death potentially transforms anything and everything. It's the single consistent fact of existence. . . . to be open to a death encounter, always means reassessing what is ultimate, significant, . . . "what counts." One asks the question of what really matters in one's life. . . . what is most life affirming and what can survive one's own death.

In the end, we are all survivors until we reach that moment when we draw our last breath. Maybe it is when we face death that we learn best how we should live.

"He who conceals his grief finds no remedy for it."

—Turkish proverb

"*In a dark time, the eye finally begins to see.*"

—Theodore Roethke

Further Reading

Lang, Monique. *Healing from Post-Traumatic Stress*. New York: McGraw-Hill, 2007.

Madgwick, Gaynor. *Aberfan: Struggling Out of Darkness*. Cardiff, Wales: Valley & Vale Community Arts, 1996.

McLean, Ian and Martin Johnes. *Aberfan: Government and Disasters*. Cardiff, Wales: Welsh Academic Press, 2000.

Milton, Ralph. *Julian's Cell: The Earthy Story of Julian of Norwich*. Kelowna, B.C.: Northstone, 2002.

Rapoport, I. C. *Aberfan: The Days After: A Journey in Pictures*. London, U.K.: Parthian Books, 2005.

Rosenbloom, Dena, Mary Beth Williams, and Barbara E. Watkins. *Life After Trauma*. New York: Guilford, 2000.

Upjohn, Sheila. *In Search of Julian of Norwich*. New York: Morehouse, 2007.

For More Information

Guilt Following Traumatic Events/
Gift from Within
  www.giftfromwithin.org/html/guilt.htm

Post-Traumatic Stress Disorder/Mayo Clinic
  www.mayoclinic.com/health/post-
  traumatic-stress-disorder/DS00246

Post-Traumatic Stress Disorder/NIMH
  www.nimh.nih.gov/health/topics/post-
  traumatic-stress-disorder-ptsd/index.
  shtml

Survivor Guilt in Holocaust Survivors
  www.holocaust-trc.org/glbsurv.htm

Why Not Me? Dealing with Survivor Guilt
  www.selfhelpmagazine.com/articles/
  trauma/guilt.html

Publisher's note:
The Web sites listed on these pages were active at the time of publication. The publisher is not responsible for Web sites that have changed their addresses or discontinued operation since the date of publication. The publisher will review and update the Web-site list upon each reprint.

Bibliography

Amery, J. *At the Mind's Limit*. New York: Schocken, 1986.

Bell, Carl C. "Cultivating Resiliency." Gift from Within—PTSD Resources for Survivors and Caregivers. www.giftfromwithin.org/html/carlbell.html.

Borg, Marcus. "Death as the Teacher of Wisdom." www.religion-online.org/showarticle.asp?title=1001.

Carlson, E. B., and C. J. Dalenberg. "A Conceptual Framework for the Impact of Traumatic Experiences." *Trauma, Violence, & Abuse*, 2000, 1, 4–28.

Caruth, Cathy. *Trauma: Explorations in Memory*. Baltimore, Md.: Johns Hopkins University Press, 1995.

The Compassionate Friends. "The Creative Use of Grief." 2000. www.tcf.org.uk/lecreative.html.

Danieli, Yael. *International Handbook of Multigenerational Legacies of Trauma*. New York: Springer, 2007.

Doka, K. A. "Act on Your Grief." *Journeys*, May 2001. At: www.hospicefoundation.org/publications/acton.htm.

Figley, C. (ed.). *Trauma and Its Wake*. New York: Bruner-Mazel, 2003.

Flood, Karen. "How to Carry On After Loss: The Guilt of the Survivor." www.abreastinthewest. ca/insight2.cfm?Num=72.

Fry, V. L. "Part of Me Died Too: Creative Strategies for Grieving Children and Adolescents," in K. J. Doka, ed. *Living with Grief: Children, Adolescents, and Loss*. Washington, D.C.: Hospice Foundation of America, 2000.

Goode, E. "Therapists Hear Survivors' Refrain: 'If only.'" *New York Times, Science Times*, November 25, 2001.

Hanawalt, Barbara. *Growing Up in Medieval London*. New York: Oxford University Press, 1993.

————. *The Ties that Bound: Peasant Families in Medieval England*. New York: Oxford University Press, 1986.

Harel, Z., B. Kahana, and E. Kahana, E. "The Effects of the Holocaust: Psychiatric, Behavioral, and Survivor Perspective." *Journal of Sociology and Social Welfare*, 1984, 11:915–929.

Hass, Aaron. "Survivor Guilt in Holocaust Survivors and Their Children." www.holocaust-trc.org/glbsurv.htm.

Bibliography

Hassan, J. "Survivors." *Community Care*. June: 11–14, 1984.

Herman, J. L. *Trauma and Recovery*. New York: Basic Books, 1992.

Jordan, M. E. "A Spiritual Perspective on Trauma and Treatment." *National Center for Post-Traumatic Stress Disorder Clinical Quarterly*, 5, 9–10.

Krystal, H. (ed.). *Massive Psychic Trauma*. New York: International Universities Press, 2003.

Langer, Lawrence. *Holocaust Testimonies: The Ruins of Memory*. New Haven, N.J.: Yale University Press, 1993.

Madgwick, Gaynor. *Aberfan: Struggling Out of Darkness*. Cardiff, Wales: Valley & Vale Community Arts, 1996.

Mayo Clinic. "Post-Traumatic Stress Disorder." www.mayoclinic.com/health/post-traumatic-stress-disorder/DS00246.

McLean, Iain and Martin Johnes. *Aberfan: Government and Disasters*. Cardiff, Wales: Welsh Academic Press, 2000.

Nader, Kathleen. "Guilt Following Traumatic Events." Gift from Within—PTSD Resources for Survivors and Caregivers. www.giftfromwithin.org/html/guilt.html.

———. "Treating Traumatic Grief in Systems." In *Death and Trauma: The Traumatology of Grieving*, edited by Charles R. Figley, Brian E. Bride, and Nicholas Mazza, 159-192. London: Taylor and Francis, 1997.

Orme, Nicholas. *Medieval Children*. New Haven, N.J.: Yale University Press, 2001.

———. *Medieval Schools*. New Haven, N. J.: Yale University Press, 2006.

Schiraldi, G. R. *The Post-Traumatic Stress Disorder Source Book*. Los Angeles: Lowell House, 2000.

Temes, Roberta. *Living with an Empty Chair: A Guide Through Grief*. Far Hills, N. J.: New Horizon Press, 1992.

Wilson, J. P. & B. Raphael (eds). *International Handbook of Traumatic Stress Syndromes*. New York: Plenum Press, 1993.

Index

Index

Picture Credits

Courtesy of Gaynor Madgwick: pp. 22, 41

Dreamstime: p. 20–21
    Broz, Karel: p. 118–119
    Haase, Andrea: p. 96–97
    Hroch, Vladimir: p. 56–57
    Wessel, Cirkel: p. 102–103

Harding House Publishing
    Ben Stewart: pp. 8, 38, 48, 58, 61, 62, 64, 66, 80, 82, 85, 88, 93, 94, 100, 104, 106, 109, 117

iStockphoto: p. 52

Jupiter Images: pp. 36–37, 78–79

Merthyr Tydfil Central Library: pp. 10, 13, 14, 17, 18, 25, 26, 42, 44, 46, 50, 68, 70–71, 86

To the best knowledge of the publisher, all images not specifically credited are in the public domain. If any image has been inadvertently uncredited, please notify Harding House Publishing Service, 220 Front Street, Vestal, New York 13850, so that credit can be given in future printings.

About the Author and the Consultant

Author

Ellyn Sanna is the author of many books. She has worked as a social worker, a teacher, an editor, and a small-business owner. She lives in New York State with her family, a couple of dogs, several goats, and a cat.

Consultant

Andrew M. Kleiman, M.D. is a Clinical Instructor in Psychiatry at New York University School of Medicine. He received a BA in philosophy from the University of Michigan, and graduated from Tulane University School of Medicine. Dr. Kleiman completed his internship, residency, and fellowship in psychiatry at New York University and Bellevue Hospital. He is currently in private practice in Manhattan and teaches at New York University School of Medicine.